AMERICAN HOLIDAYS
THE FOURTH OF JULY

KIM THOMPSON

NORWOOD HOUSE PRESS

Cataloging-in-Publication Data

Names: Thompson, Kim.
Title: The Fourth of July / Kim Thompson.
Description: Buffalo, NY : Norwood House Press, 2026. | Series: American holidays | Includes glossary and index.
Identifiers: ISBN 9781978575257 (pbk.) | ISBN 9781978575264 (library bound) | ISBN 9781978575271 (ebook)
Subjects: LCSH: Fourth of July--Juvenile literature. | Fourth of July celebrations--Juvenile literature.
Classification: LCC E286.T466 2026 | DDC 394.2634--dc23

Published in 2026 by
Norwood House Press
2544 Clinton Street
Buffalo, NY 14224

Copyright © 2026 Norwood House Press
Designer: Rhea Magaro

Photo credits: Cover, p.1 Christin Lola/Shutterstock.com; pp. 4, 7, 8, 10, 11 Library of Congress; p. 6 Stuart, Gilbert/Shutterstock.com; p. 8 P&P/Shutterstock.com; p. 9 Sheila Fitzgerald/Shutterstock.com; p. 5, 12-15 Wiki; p. 16 Janson George/Shutterstock.com; p. 17 jfergusonphotos/Shutterstock.com; p. 18 Monkey Business Images/Shutterstock.com; p. 19 Freebilly Photography/Shutterstock.com; p. 21 sonya etchison/Shutterstock.com;

All rights reserved. No part of this book may be reproduced in any form without permission in writing from the publisher, except by a reviewer.

Printed in the United States of America

Some of the images in this book illustrate individuals who are models. The depictions do not imply actual situations or events.

CPSIA compliance information: Batch #CSNHP26: For further information contact Norwood House Press at 1-800-237-9932.

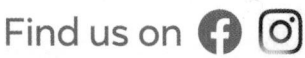

TABLE OF CONTENTS

How It Began 4

A Declaration 10

A National Holiday 16

Happy Birthday, America! 20

Glossary 22

Thinking Questions 23

Index 24

About the Author 24

HOW IT BEGAN

About 250 years ago, the United States was not a country. It was a group of 13 **colonies**. The colonies were ruled by the country of Great Britain.

Everything changed on July 4, 1776. On that day, Americans decided to break away from Great Britain. They made a new, free country.

John Adams was an early American leader. In 1776, he wrote to his wife. He predicted that Americans would have a day of celebration every year in July.

Adams wrote that the day would be for "**pomp** and parade, with shows, games, sports, guns, bells, bonfires, and **illuminations**...from this time forward forever more."

John Adams was right. Ever since 1776, Americans have celebrated on July 4th.

The holiday is called the Fourth of July. It is also called **Independence** Day.

A DECLARATION

Over 400 years ago, people began to cross the ocean on ships to come to North America. Many came from Great Britain.

These **colonists** lived far away from Great Britain. But they still had to follow Great Britain's laws. They still had to pay the British king.

The colonists liked their new home. They wanted to make their own rules. They got angrier and angrier.

Finally, they decided to fight. Starting in 1775, they fought the Revolutionary War against Great Britain. A few years later, they won.

Thomas Jefferson and other leaders wrote a **document**. It was called the **Declaration** of Independence. It said that the colonies were no longer part of Great Britain. It said that Americans wanted, "life, **liberty**, and the **pursuit** of happiness."

On July 4, 1776, leaders voted to approve the Declaration of Independence. The new country of the United States of America was born.

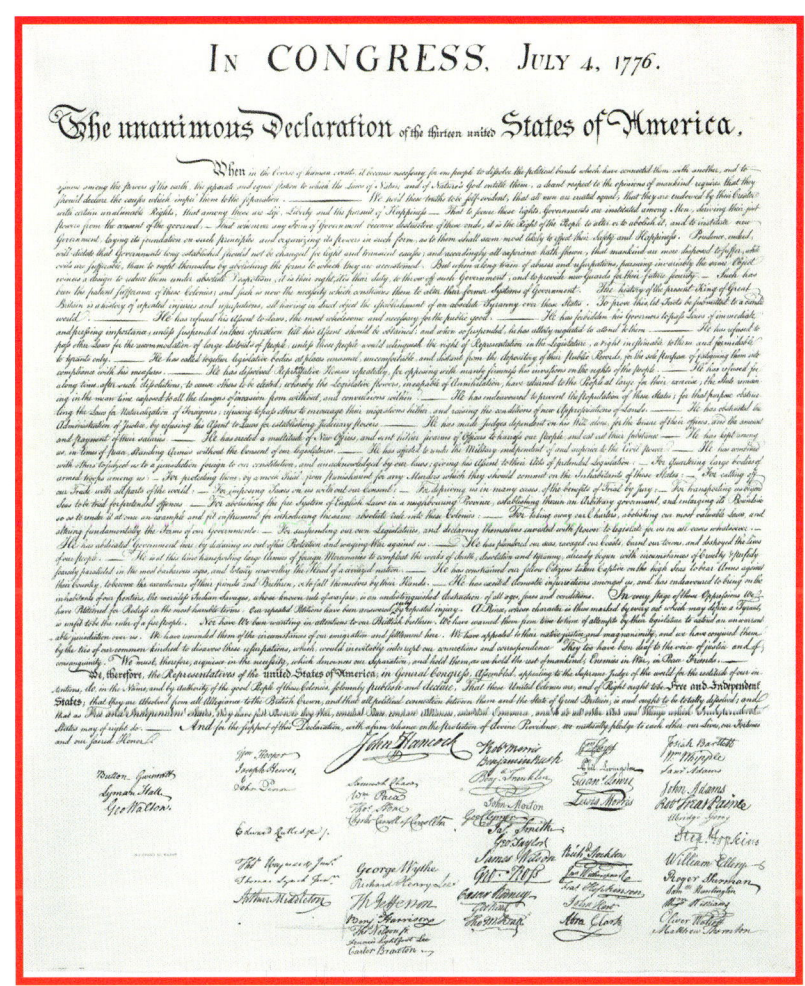

A NATIONAL HOLIDAY

The Fourth of July is a national holiday. Many adults get the day off work. Americans celebrate all day long.

In the morning, many towns have parades. People wave American flags. American soldiers wear their uniforms proudly. Bands play **patriotic** songs.

In the afternoon, families and friends have picnics. They eat hot dogs, corn on the cob, and other American foods. Some people go to baseball stadiums to watch "America's game."

As the sun goes down, people gather in parks and fields. Radio stations play "The Star-Spangled Banner" and other American songs. Soon, fireworks begin. The exploding lights are red, white, and blue. The crowds cheer!

HAPPY BIRTHDAY, AMERICA!

On the Fourth of July, Americans celebrate their nation's birthday. They remember all those who fought to make their country free.

GLOSSARY

colonies (KAH-luh-neez): territories that have been settled by people from another country and that are also controlled by that country

colonists (KAH-luh-nists): people who live in a colony, or a territory that was settled by people from another country and is controlled by that country

declaration (dek-luh-RAY-shuhn): an announcement

document (DAHK-yuh-muhnt): a piece of paper containing official information

illuminations (i-loo-muh-NAY-shuhnz): things that are lit up

independence (in-di-PEN-duhns): freedom; self-rule

liberty (LIB-ur-tee): freedom

patriotic (pay-tree-AH-tik): full of loyalty and love for a country

pomp (pahmp): a fancy, official display

pursuit (pur-SOOT): a chase or quest to find something

THINKING QUESTIONS

1. What did John Adams predict?

2. Why did colonists fight in the Revolutionary War?

3. What did the Declaration of Independence declare?

4. On what date was the Declaration of Independence approved?

5. Name three ways that Americans celebrate the Fourth of July.

INDEX

Adams, John 6–8

colonies 4, 14

Declaration of Independence 14, 15

fireworks 19

flags 17

Great Britain 4, 5, 10, 11, 13, 14

Jefferson, Thomas 14

parades 7, 17

picnics 18

Revolutionary War 13

soldiers 17

songs 17, 19

ABOUT THE AUTHOR

Kim Thompson is a teacher and writer from Columbus, Ohio. She is grateful to all those who have fought to make our country free. She loves to celebrate the Fourth of July by sitting in the grass with other Americans and saying "oooh" and "ahhh" as fireworks go off overhead.